Introduction

Welcome to "Python Programming for Beginners," a comprehensive guide designed to introduce you to the world of programming through Python. My name is Nitin Bhatia, and with over 18 years of experience in both the tech industry and management, I have had the privilege of witnessing and contributing to the rapid evolution of technology. Throughout my career, I have seen firsthand the transformative power of programming and the myriad of opportunities it can unlock.

Python has emerged as one of the most popular and versatile programming languages, renowned for its simplicity and readability. Whether you are a student, a working professional looking to enhance your skill set, or simply someone with a curiosity for coding, this book is crafted to guide you from the basics to more advanced concepts in a structured and engaging manner. My goal is to provide you with a solid foundation in Python, enabling you to build your own projects and solve real-world problems with confidence.

Preface

This book is dedicated to my beloved wife, Richa, and our wonderful daughter, Vaanya. Their unwavering support and encouragement have been the driving force behind this endeavor. Richa, your patience and belief in my vision have been my constant source of strength. Vaanya, your curiosity and enthusiasm for learning inspire me every day to be a better teacher and father.

Over the past 18 years, I have had the opportunity to work in various roles within the tech industry and management. These experiences have enriched my understanding of how technology can be leveraged to create impactful solutions. Through this book, I aim to share the knowledge and insights I have gathered, presenting them in a way that is accessible and enjoyable for beginners.

The journey of learning Python is both exciting and rewarding. Each chapter is designed to build on the previous one, ensuring a smooth and logical progression through the topics. You will find practical examples, exercises, and projects that reinforce your understanding and help you apply what you have learned.

As you embark on this journey, remember that learning to code is a process that requires patience and persistence. Embrace the challenges and celebrate your progress. I hope this book serves as a valuable resource in your path to mastering Python and opens up new possibilities for you in the world of programming.

Thank you for choosing this book. Let's begin this exciting adventure together.

....Nitin

INDEX

Module 1: Getting Started

1. Introduction to Programming
   - What is programming?
   - History of Python
   - Applications of Python

2. Setting Up the Environment
   - Installing Python
   - Introduction to Integrated Development Environments (IDEs)
   - Setting up IDE (e.g., PyCharm, VS Code)

3. Writing Your First Python Program
   - Understanding the basic syntax
   - Running a Python script
   - Writing a simple "Hello, World!" program

Module 2: Basic Python Syntax

1. Variables and Data Types
   - Introduction to variables
   - Common data types: integers, floats, strings, booleans
   - Type conversion

2. Operators
   - Arithmetic operators
   - Comparison operators
   - Logical operators
   - Assignment operators

3. Input and Output
   - Getting user input
   - Displaying output

Module 3: Control Structures

1. Conditional Statements
   - if, else, elif statements
   - Nested conditions

2. Loops
   - while loop
   - for loop
   - Loop control statements: break, continue, pass

Module 4: Functions

1. Defining Functions
   - Function syntax
   - Parameters and arguments
   - Return values

2. Scope and Lifetime of Variables
   - Local vs. global variables
   - Variable scope

3. Built-in Functions vs. User-defined Functions
   - Using built-in functions
   - Creating custom functions

Module 5: Data Structures

1. Lists
   - Creating lists
   - Accessing and modifying list elements
   - Common list methods

2. Tuples
   - Creating tuples
   - Accessing tuple elements
   - Immutable nature of tuples

3. Dictionaries
   - Creating dictionaries
   - Accessing and modifying dictionary values
   - Dictionary methods

4. Sets
   - Creating sets
   - Set operations

Module 6: Working with Strings

1. String Manipulation
   - String indexing and slicing
   - Common string methods
   - String formatting

2. Regular Expressions (Optional Advanced Topic)
   - Introduction to regular expressions
   - Using the re module

Module 7: File Handling

1. Reading and Writing Files
   - Opening and closing files
   - Reading from a file
   - Writing to a file

2. Working with Different File Types
   - Text files
   - CSV files

Module 8: Error Handling

1. Exceptions and Error Handling
   - Understanding exceptions
   - try, except, finally blocks
   - Raising exceptions

Module 9: Modules and Packages

1. Introduction to Modules
   - Importing modules
   - Standard library modules

2. Creating and Using Packages
   - Creating your own modules
   - Organizing code with packages

Module 10: Introduction to Object-Oriented Programming (OOP)

1. Basic Concepts
   - Classes and objects
   - Attributes and methods

2. Advanced OOP Concepts
   - Inheritance
   - Polymorphism
   - Encapsulation

Module 11: Working with Libraries and Frameworks

1. Popular Libraries
   - NumPy for numerical computations
   - Pandas for data analysis
   - Matplotlib for data visualization

2. Introduction to Web Frameworks (Optional Advanced Topic)
   - Flask for web development
   - Django basics

Module 12: Project-Based Learning

1. Building a Simple Project
   - Project planning and design
   - Coding the project
   - Testing and debugging

2. Capstone Project
   - Choose a project that combines various concepts learned
   - Project development and presentation

Bonus Chapter 1: Practice Exercises for Python Code Beginners

Bonus Chapter 2: Python Certification Prep Questions

Conclusion

1. Review of Key Concepts
   - Summarizing key points
   - Reinforcing understanding

2. Next Steps
   - Further learning resources
   - Introduction to advanced topics and specializations

Additional Resources

1. Reference Materials
   - Recommended books
   - Online resources and communities

2. Practice Exercises
   - Coding challenges
   - Real-world scenarios

Module 1: Getting Started

1. Introduction to Programming

What is Programming?

Think of your computer as a very obedient but not-so-smart assistant. It can do amazing things, but only if you give it very clear instructions. Programming is the process of giving these instructions, written in a special language that the computer understands. For example, if you wanted your assistant to make a sandwich, you would need to tell them exactly how to do it step by step.

History of Python

Python is a popular programming language created by Guido van Rossum in the late 1980s and released in 1991. He wanted a language that was easy to read and simple to use, which is why Python's syntax looks like plain English. The name "Python" comes from the British comedy series "Monty Python's Flying Circus," which Guido enjoyed.

Applications of Python

Python is used in many different fields:

- **Web Development:** Websites like YouTube and Instagram are built using Python.
- **Data Analysis:** Companies use Python to analyze data and make decisions. For example, Netflix uses Python to recommend movies and shows to you.
- **Artificial Intelligence:** Python is used to create intelligent systems, like self-driving cars and virtual assistants such as Siri.
- **Game Development:** Some video games are developed using Python, making it possible to create fun and interactive experiences.

2. Setting Up the Environment

Installing Python

1. Go to the official Python website.
2. Download the latest version suitable for your operating system (Windows, Mac).
3. Follow the installation instructions provided on the website.

Introduction to Integrated Development Environments (IDEs)

An IDE is like a special notebook where you write your code. It helps you write, test, and fix your code easily. Some popular IDEs for Python are:

- PyCharm: Great for beginners and has many helpful features.
- Visual Studio Code (VS Code): A versatile and lightweight option.

Setting Up an IDE

- Download and install PyCharm or VS Code from their official websites.
- Open the IDE and create a new project or file.
- Write a simple Python script and run it to make sure everything is set up correctly.

3. Writing Your First Python Program

Understanding the Basic Syntax

Python syntax is straightforward and readable. Here's an example:

```
# This is a comment
print("Hello, World!")
```

Run the script in your IDE to see the output "Hello, World!" displayed

This code uses the print() function to display the text inside the parentheses.

By the end of Module 1, you'll understand the basics of programming, know a bit about Python's history and its applications, and have practical experience setting up your coding environment and writing your first program.

Module 2: Basic Python Syntax

Variables and Data Types

1. Introduction to Variables

Think of variables as containers that hold information. Just like you might use a lunchbox to carry your sandwich, a variable can hold different types of data in Python.

Example: Imagine you have a box labeled "snacks." You can put different types of snacks like apples, cookies, or chips in the box. Similarly, a variable named snacks can hold different types of data like numbers, words, or even true/false statements.

2. Common Data Types

Integers

Integers are whole numbers without any decimals. They can be positive or negative.
Example: Your age, the number of books on a shelf, or the temperature outside.

Floats

Floats are numbers with decimals. They represent values that are not whole numbers.
Example: The price of a product, your weight, or the height of a building.

Strings

Strings are sequences of characters, such as letters, numbers, or symbols, enclosed within quotes.
Example: Your name, a sentence, or a website URL.

Booleans

Booleans represent two values: True or False. They're often used for making decisions in programming.
Example: It's raining outside (True/False), or you have a pet (True/False).

3. Type Conversion

Sometimes you need to convert data from one type to another. For example, turning a string into a number or vice versa.
Example: Converting the string "10" into the integer 10, or turning the number 5 into the string "5".

Operators

1. Arithmetic Operators

Arithmetic operators are used to perform mathematical operations like addition, subtraction, multiplication, and division.
Example: Adding two numbers (5 + 3), subtracting (10 - 4), multiplying (6 * 2), or dividing (8 / 2).

2. Comparison Operators

Comparison operators are used to compare values and return True or False.
Example: Checking if two numbers are equal (5 == 5), or if one number is greater than another (10 > 5).

3. Logical Operators

Logical operators are used to combine conditional statements.
Example: Checking if both conditions are true (True and True), or if at least one condition is true (True or False).

4. Assignment Operators

Assignment operators are used to assign values to variables.
Example: Assigning a value to a variable (x = 5), or updating the value of a variable (x += 2).

Input and Output

1. Getting User Input

You can ask the user to enter data using the input() function.

```python
name = input("What's your name? ")
print("Hello, " + name + "!")
```

In this example, the input() function prompts the user to enter their name, which is then stored in the variable name. The print() function displays a personalized greeting using the entered name.

2. Displaying Output

You can use the print() function to display information to the user.

```python
age = 25
print("I am", age, "years old.")
```

Here, the print() function outputs the message "I am 25 years old." The value of the variable age is inserted into the message using commas to separate the different parts.

Now that we've covered the basic syntax of Python, we can start writing our own programs and experimenting with different concepts. Remember, practice makes perfect, so don't hesitate to try out different examples and explore the capabilities of Python!

Module 3: Control Structures

In Module 3, we'll explore control structures in Python, which allow us to make decisions and control the flow of our programs.

Conditional Statements

Conditional statements are like forks in the road, where the direction taken depends on certain conditions.

1. if, else, elseif Statements

Think of if statements like making decisions in real life. For example, if it's raining, you might take an umbrella; otherwise, you won't need it. Similarly, in Python:

```python
weather = "rainy"
if weather == "rainy":
    print("Take an umbrella!")
else:
    print("No need for an umbrella.")
```

2. Nested Conditions

Nested conditions are like opening a box within another box. You might have a decision tree where each choice leads to more options. In Python, it looks something like this:

```python
weather = "sunny"
time = "morning"

if weather == "sunny":
    if time == "morning":
        print("It's a beautiful morning!")
    else:
        print("Enjoy the sunshine!")
else:
    print("It's not sunny today.")
```

Loops

Loops help us repeat actions without having to write the same code multiple times.

1. while Loop

A while loop is like a marathon runner. They keep running until they reach the finish line or a certain condition is met. For example:

```python
count = 0
while count < 5:
    print("Counting:", count)
    count += 1
```

2. for Loop

A for loop is like going through a shopping list. You go through each item until you've checked everything off. For example:

```python
shopping_list = ["apples", "bananas", "oranges"]
for item in shopping_list:
    print("Buy", item)
```

3. Loop Control Statements: break, continue, pass

- **break**: Stops the loop entirely, like an emergency stop button.
- **continue**: Skips the current iteration and moves to the next one, like pressing the snooze button.
- **pass**: Does nothing, just moves to the next line of code, like waiting for the green light at a traffic signal.

Let's go into more detailed explanation:

Break: Imagine you're searching for a specific toy in a toy store. As soon as you find it, you break out of the store because you don't need to keep searching. Similarly, in Python:

```python
toys = ["car", "doll", "puzzle", "teddy"]
for toy in toys:
    if toy == "puzzle":
        print("Puzzle found! Breaking out of the store!")
        break
    print("Searching for", toy)
```

Continue: Picture yourself in a candy store with different types of candies. You love chocolates, so whenever you see any other candy, you skip it and move to the next one. In Python:

```python
candies = ["chocolate", "lollipop", "gummy bear", "toffee"]
for candy in candies:
    if candy != "chocolate":
        print("Not interested in", candy, "Skipping to the next one!")
        continue
    print("Yay! I found chocolate!")
```

Pass: Consider you're in a dance class, and the instructor asks you to perform a step you're not familiar with. Instead of freezing, you simply pass and move on to the next step. In Python:

```python
dance_steps = ["salsa", "waltz", "rumba", "tango"]
for step in dance_steps:
    if step == "rumba":
        print("I don't know how to do the rumba! Passing...")
        pass
    print("Performing", step)
```

Module 4: Functions

Welcome, Python enthusiasts! In Module 4, we'll embark on an exciting journey into the realm of functions. Functions are like magical spells in the world of programming. They encapsulate a set of instructions that perform a specific task and can be reused throughout your code.

1. Defining Functions

Imagine you're a chef in a bustling restaurant. Just like how you create recipes to make delicious dishes, in Python, we define functions to perform specific tasks. For example, you might have a function called make_pizza() that contains instructions for creating a mouthwatering pizza.

Function Syntax

In Python, defining a function is easy-peasy! It starts with the def keyword followed by the function name and parentheses. Inside the parentheses, you can specify parameters if needed. Then, the function body, enclosed in curly braces, contains the instructions for the task.

```python
def make_pizza():
    print("Roll out the dough")
    print("Add toppings")
    print("Bake in the oven")
```

2. Parameters and Arguments

In our restaurant analogy, parameters are like ingredients. When you define a function, you can specify parameters to accept input data. For instance, in our make_pizza() function, you might have parameters like toppings or size.

```python
def make_pizza(toppings, size):
    print(f"Making a {size} pizza with {toppings}")
```

When you call the function, you provide arguments, which are the actual values passed into the function.

```python
make_pizza("pepperoni", "large")
```

3. Return Values

After cooking up a storm in the kitchen (or running our function), we often want something in return. That's where return values come in! They allow a function to send data back to the caller.

```python
def square(number):
    return number ** 2

result = square(5)
print(result)  # Output: 25
```

4. Scope and Lifetime of Variables

Imagine you have different ingredient containers in your kitchen. Some are accessible anywhere (global variables), while others are only available within specific recipes (local variables).

Local vs. Global Variables

Local variables are like ingredients used within a specific recipe, while global variables are like pantry staples accessible to all recipes.

```python
# Global variable
pantry_staple = "flour"

def make_pizza():
    # Local variable
    topping = "cheese"
    print(f"Using {pantry_staple} and {topping} to make pizza")

make_pizza()
print(f"Using {pantry_staple} to bake bread")
```

In this example, pantry_staple is a global variable accessible throughout the code, while topping is a local variable available only within the make_pizza() function.

5. Built-in Functions vs. User-defined Functions

Python provides a treasure trove of built-in functions, ready to use at your fingertips. However, sometimes you need to create your own custom functions tailored to your specific needs.

Using Built-in Functions

Just like grabbing pre-packaged ingredients from the store, built-in functions allow you to perform common tasks without reinventing the wheel.

```python
# Built-in functions
print(len("hello"))  # Output: 5
print(max(5, 10, 3))  # Output: 10
```

Creating Custom Functions

But what if you have a secret family recipe for the best spaghetti sauce? That's where custom functions come in handy! You can encapsulate your special sauce-making instructions into a function and reuse them whenever you want to impress your dinner guests.

```python
# Custom function
def make_spaghetti_sauce():
    print("Step 1: Saute onions and garlic")
    print("Step 2: Add tomatoes and herbs")
    print("Step 3: Simmer until delicious")

make_spaghetti_sauce()
```

And there you have it, adventurers! You've unlocked the power of functions in Python. Now go forth and create magical code spells to conquer the programming world!

Module 5: Data Structures

Welcome to Module 5! In this module, we'll dive into the fascinating world of data structures. Think of data structures as containers that allow you to organize and manipulate your data efficiently. We'll explore four essential data structures in Python: Lists, Tuples, Dictionaries, and Sets.

1. Lists:

- **Creating Lists:** Imagine you're planning a picnic and need to make a list of items to bring, like sandwiches, drinks, and snacks. You can create a list in Python using square brackets [ ].

- **Accessing and Modifying List Elements:** Suppose you've made your picnic list, but now you want to add more items or change the existing ones. You can access and modify list elements using their index.

- **Common List Methods:** Python provides several built-in methods to work with lists. For example, append() adds an item to the end of the list, remove() deletes a specific item, and sort() arranges the items in ascending order.

```python
# Example of list creation and modification
picnic_list = ["sandwiches", "drinks", "snacks"]
picnic_list.append("fruits")  # Adding fruits to the list
picnic_list[1] = "juice"  # Changing drinks to juice
```

2. Tuples:

- **Creating Tuples:** Let's say you're organizing a concert and want to store the performers' names and their genres. Tuples are similar to lists but are immutable, meaning their values cannot be changed after creation. You create tuples using parentheses ( ).

- **Accessing Tuple Elements:** Once you've created a tuple, you can access its elements using indexing, just like lists.

- **Immutable Nature of Tuples:** Unlike lists, you cannot modify tuple elements after creation. This immutability makes tuples useful for storing data that should not be changed.

```python
# Example of tuple creation
performers = ("Taylor Swift", "Pop")
```

3. Dictionaries:

- **Creating Dictionaries:** Imagine you're building a contact book where each entry consists of a name and phone number. Dictionaries in Python allow you to store data in key-value pairs, enclosed in curly braces { }.

- **Accessing and Modifying Dictionary Values:** You can access dictionary values using their keys and modify them as needed.

- **Dictionary Methods:** Python offers various methods to manipulate dictionaries. For instance, keys() returns all the keys, values() returns all the values, and items() returns key-value pairs.

```python
# Example of dictionary creation and modification
contact_book = {"Alice": 12345, "Bob": 67890}
contact_book["Charlie"] = 24680  # Adding Charlie to the contact book
```

4. Sets:

- **Creating Sets:** Suppose you're organizing a team-building event and want to keep track of the participants. Sets are collections of unique elements, perfect for this scenario.

- **Set Operations:** You can perform various operations on sets, such as union, intersection, difference, and symmetric difference.

```python
# Example of set creation and operations
participants = {"Alice", "Bob", "Charlie"}
new_participants = {"Bob", "David", "Eve"}
all_participants = participants.union(new_participants)  # Combining both sets
```

That concludes our exploration of data structures in Python. Remember to practice coding with these structures to solidify your understanding. Happy coding!

Module 6: Working with Strings

Welcome to Module 6! Today, we'll embark on an exciting journey into the world of strings. Strings are not just sequences of characters; they're powerful tools for manipulating text data. Get ready to dive in and explore various aspects of string manipulation, including indexing, slicing, common methods, string formatting, and even a sneak peek into regular expressions!

1. **String Manipulation:** Strings are like digital clay that we can shape to our will. Imagine you have a sentence, and you want to capitalize it. With string manipulation, you can achieve that and much more!

2. **String Indexing and Slicing:** Think of strings as a lineup of characters, each with its own number. Indexing allows you to pinpoint specific characters or ranges of characters within a string. Slicing lets you extract substrings based on their positions.

3. **Common String Methods:** Python provides a treasure trove of built-in methods to manipulate strings. From converting cases to searching for substrings and replacing text, these methods make string manipulation a breeze.

```
# Example of common string methods
text = "hello, world!"
print(text.upper())  # Output: HELLO, WORLD!
print(text.replace("hello", "hi"))  # Output: hi, world!
```

4. **String Formatting:** Formatting strings is like dressing them up for a party! Python offers various ways to format strings, including the format() method and f-strings, allowing you to inject variables and expressions into strings seamlessly.

```
# Example of string formatting
name = "Alice"
age = 30
print(f"My name is {name} and I am {age} years old.")
```

5. **Regular Expressions (Optional Advanced Topic):** Regular expressions are like wizards that wield powerful spells to manipulate text with precision. While optional, learning about regular expressions opens doors to advanced string manipulation techniques.

```
# Example of using regular expressions
import re
text = "The cat sat on the mat."
matches = re.findall(r"\b\w{3}\b", text)  # Find 3-letter words
print(matches)  # Output: ['The', 'cat', 'sat', 'the']
```

Get ready to level up your string skills and unleash your creativity with these powerful tools! Let's dive in and have some fun with strings!

Module 7: File Handling

Welcome to Module 7! Today, we're diving into the exciting world of file handling. Imagine you have a magic bookshelf where you can store and retrieve different types of books. Well, in Python, file handling is like interacting with that magical bookshelf!

1. **Reading and Writing Files:** Think of files as containers for storing information. You can read data from files or write new information into them. It's like reading a story from a book or adding your own chapter to it!

2. **Opening and Closing Files:** Before you can read or write to a file, you need to open it. Opening a file is like unlocking a treasure chest to access its contents. And when you're done, you should always close the file to save resources and ensure everything stays tidy.

```python
# Example of opening and closing a file
file = open("my_file.txt", "r")
content = file.read()
print(content)
file.close()
```

3. **Reading from a File:** Reading from a file allows you to access the information stored within it. It's like flipping through the pages of a book to see what's written inside. You can read the entire file at once or line by line.

```python
# Example of reading from a file
with open("my_file.txt", "r") as file:
    for line in file:
        print(line.strip())  # Strip removes extra spaces and newlines
```

4. **Writing to a File:** Writing to a file lets you add new content or overwrite existing information. It's like adding your thoughts to a journal or updating a recipe book with your latest culinary creations.

```python
# Example of writing to a file
with open("my_file.txt", "w") as file:
    file.write("Hello, world!\n")
    file.write("This is a new line.")
```

5. **Working with Different File Types:** In the world of files, there are different types, just like there are different genres of books. We'll focus on two common types: text files, which store plain text, and CSV files, which organize data into rows and columns.

Let's embark on this magical journey into the world of file handling together!

Module 8: Error Handling

Welcome to Module 8 of our course! In this module, we'll delve into the fascinating world of error handling. Just like in real life, where unexpected things can happen, in programming, errors can occur too. But fear not! With the power of error handling, we can gracefully handle these unforeseen situations and keep our programs running smoothly.

Section 1: Understanding Exceptions

What are Exceptions?

Imagine you're baking a cake. You follow the recipe meticulously, but suddenly you realize you're out of eggs! This unexpected situation is like an exception in programming. An exception is an event that disrupts the normal flow of a program's execution.

Common Types of Exceptions

1. **SyntaxError:** This occurs when the code violates the syntax rules of the programming language. It's like trying to bake a cake without following the recipe properly.

2. **TypeError:** This occurs when an operation is performed on a variable of an inappropriate data type. It's like trying to use a spoon to cut a cake—it's just not the right tool for the job!

3. **ZeroDivisionError:** This occurs when you try to divide a number by zero. It's like trying to divide a cake into zero pieces—you'll end up with an error!

How to Handle Exceptions

Now, let's learn how to handle these exceptions using Python's try, except, and finally blocks.

Section 2: try, except, finally Blocks

The try Block

The try block is where you place the code that might raise an exception. It's like attempting to bake the cake according to the recipe.

```
try:
    # Code that might raise an exception
    print(5 / 0)  # Trying to divide by zero
except:
    print("An error occurred!")
```

The except Block

The except block is where you handle the exception that was raised in the try block. It's like improvising when you realize you're out of eggs while baking the cake.

```
try:
    print(5 / 0)
except ZeroDivisionError:
    print("Cannot divide by zero!")
```

The finally Block

The finally block is executed regardless of whether an exception occurred or not. It's like cleaning up the kitchen after baking the cake, no matter the outcome.

```
try:
    print(5 / 0)
except ZeroDivisionError:
    print("Cannot divide by zero!")
finally:
    print("Cleaning up...")
```

Section 3: Raising Exceptions

What is Raising an Exception?

Sometimes, you might want to trigger an exception manually. This is called raising an exception. It's like declaring that your cake batter has gone bad and you can't proceed with baking.

How to Raise an Exception

You can raise an exception using the raise keyword followed by the type of exception you want to raise.

```
def greet(name):
    if not isinstance(name, str):
        raise TypeError("Name must be a string!")
    print(f"Hello, {name}!")

greet(100)  # This will raise a TypeError
```

Conclusion

Congratulations! You've completed Module 8 on error handling. You now understand how exceptions work, how to handle them using try, except, and finally blocks, and how to raise exceptions when needed. Just like a master chef who can adapt to any kitchen mishaps, you're now equipped to handle any errors that come your way in Python programming. Keep coding and happy error handling!

Module 9: Modules and Packages

Welcome to Module 9 of our Python programming course! In this module, we'll explore the fascinating world of modules and packages. Just like in real life, where we organize our belongings into different categories and packages for easy access, in programming, we use modules and packages to organize our code and make it reusable and maintainable.

Section 1: Introduction to Modules

What are Modules?

Imagine you have a toolbox filled with various tools for different tasks. Each tool serves a specific purpose, and you can easily access them when needed. Similarly, in Python, a module is a file containing Python code that defines functions, classes, and variables. It's like a toolbox for our Python programs!

Benefits of Using Modules

1. **Code Reusability:** Modules allow us to reuse code across different parts of our program or even in different programs altogether. This saves time and promotes code efficiency.
2. **Organized Code:** By organizing related functions and classes into modules, we can keep our codebase clean and maintainable. It's like having separate compartments in our toolbox for different types of tools.

Example: Using a Module

Let's say we have a module named math_operations.py that contains functions for performing mathematical operations. We can import this module into our Python script and use its functions.

```
# math_operations.py
def add(a, b):
    return a + b


def subtract(a, b):
    return a - b


# main.py
import math_operations

result = math_operations.add(5, 3)
print(result)  # Output: 8
```

Section 2: Importing Modules

How to Import Modules
Python provides several ways to import modules into our scripts:

1. **import:** This is the most common way to import a module. It imports the entire module namespace, and we access its functions and classes using dot notation.

```
import math_operations
result = math_operations.add(5, 3)
```

2. **from ... import:** This method allows us to import specific functions or classes from a module directly into our script's namespace, eliminating the need for dot notation.

```
from math_operations import add
result = add(5, 3)
```

3. **import ... as ...:** This syntax allows us to import a module with an alias, making it easier to refer to in our code.

```
import math_operations as math_ops
result = math_ops.add(5, 3)
```

Standard Library Modules

Python comes with a vast standard library that contains modules for various purposes, such as mathematics, file handling, networking, and more. These modules are readily available for use without the need for installation.

Example: Using Standard Library Modules

Let's say we want to generate random numbers in our Python script. We can use the `random` module from the Python standard library.

```
import random
random_number = random.randint(1, 100)
print(random_number)
```

Section 3: Creating and Using Packages

What are Packages?

Just like how we organize our tools into toolboxes and then into larger containers for better organization, in Python, we organize our modules into packages. A package is a directory that contains Python modules and a special file named __init__.py. It allows us to structure our code into hierarchical namespaces.

Example: Creating a Package

Let's say we want to create a package named utilities that contains modules for common utility functions. We'll create the following directory structure:

```
utilities/
    __init__.py
    math_operations.py
    string_operations.py
```

Now, we can import modules from the utilities package into our Python scripts.

```python
from utilities import math_operations
result = math_operations.add(5, 3)
print(result)
```

Organizing Code with Packages

By organizing our code into packages, we can maintain a clear and structured codebase, making it easier to navigate and understand. Packages also facilitate code sharing and collaboration among team members.

Conclusion

Congratulations! You've completed Module 9 on modules and packages in Python. You now understand the importance of organizing code using modules and packages, how to import modules into your scripts, and how to create your own packages. With this knowledge, you'll be able to write more organized, reusable, and maintainable Python code. Keep coding and exploring the vast world of Python programming!

Module 10: Introduction to Object-Oriented Programming (OOP)

Welcome to Module 10 of our Python programming adventure! In this module, we'll embark on a journey to explore the magical world of Object-Oriented Programming (OOP). Get ready to dive into the world of classes, objects, inheritance, polymorphism, encapsulation, and more! But fear not, we'll make learning fun and engaging with real-world examples and interactive code snippets.

Section 1: Basic Concepts

1.1 Classes and Objects

Imagine you're in a magical workshop where you can create your own creatures. In this workshop, a class is like a blueprint that describes what each creature will look like and how it will behave. Let's create a simple class called Creature:

```python
class Creature:
    def __init__(self, name, species):
        self.name = name
        self.species = species

    def greet(self):
        return f"Hello! I'm {self.name}, a {self.species}."
```

Now, let's use this blueprint to create our first creature:

```python
my_pet = Creature("Fluffy", "Cat")
print(my_pet.greet())  # Output: Hello! I'm Fluffy, a Cat.
```

Here, my_pet is an object of the Creature class.

1.2 Attributes and Methods

In our magical workshop, each creature can have unique characteristics (attributes) and abilities (methods). Let's add some attributes and methods to our Creature class:

```python
class Creature:
    def __init__(self, name, species, color):
        self.name = name
        self.species = species
        self.color = color

    def greet(self):
        return f"Hello! I'm {self.name}, a {self.color} {self.species}."

    def change_color(self, new_color):
        self.color = new_color
```

Now, our creatures can change their colors:

```python
my_pet = Creature("Fluffy", "Cat", "Brown")
print(my_pet.greet()) # Output: Hello! I'm Fluffy, a Brown Cat.
my_pet.change_color("White")
print(my_pet.greet()) # Output: Hello! I'm Fluffy, a White Cat.
```

Section 2: Advanced OOP Concepts

2.1 Inheritance

Inheritance allows creatures to inherit traits from their ancestors. Let's create a subclass called Dog that inherits from Creature:

```python
class Dog(Creature):
    def bark(self):
        return "Woof! Woof!"
```

Now, our Dog inherits the greet() method from Creature and gains its own bark() method:

```python
my_dog = Dog("Buddy", "Dog", "Golden")
print(my_dog.greet()) # Output: Hello! I'm Buddy, a Golden Dog.
print(my_dog.bark()) # Output: Woof! Woof!
```

2.2 Polymorphism

Polymorphism allows creatures to perform the same action in different ways. Let's add a speak() method to both Creature and Dog:

```python
class Creature:
    # Previous code...

    def speak(self):
        return "Hello!"

class Dog(Creature):
    # Previous code...

    def speak(self):
        return "Woof! Woof!"
```

Now, our creatures can speak, each in their own way:

```python
print(my_pet.speak()) # Output: Hello!
print(my_dog.speak()) # Output: Woof! Woof!
```

2.3 Encapsulation

Encapsulation hides the internal details of a creature from the outside world. Let's make the color attribute of our creatures private:

```python
class Creature:
    def __init__(self, name, species, color):
        self.name = name
        self.species = species
        self.__color = color  # Private attribute

    def greet(self):
        return f"Hello! I'm {self.name}, a {self.__color} {self.species}."

    def change_color(self, new_color):
        self.__color = new_color
```

Now, the color attribute can only be accessed and modified within the class:

```python
print(my_pet.__color)  # Error: AttributeError: 'Creature' object has no attribute '__color'
```

Conclusion

Congratulations! You've completed Module 10 on Object-Oriented Programming (OOP). You've learned how to create classes, objects, inheritance, polymorphism, and encapsulation using Python. Now, go forth and create your own magical creatures and adventures in the realm of programming!

Module 11: Working with Libraries and Frameworks

Welcome to Module 11 of our Python adventure! In this module, we'll explore the exciting world of libraries and frameworks that extend the capabilities of Python and make our lives as developers easier. Get ready to dive into numerical computations, data analysis, visualization, and even web development using popular tools like NumPy, Pandas, Matplotlib, Flask, and Django. Let's embark on this journey together and discover how these tools can revolutionize the way we work with Python!

Section 1: Popular Libraries

1.1 NumPy for Numerical Computations

Imagine you're a scientist analyzing vast amounts of numerical data from experiments. You need a powerful tool to handle these computations efficiently. That's where NumPy comes in handy! NumPy is a fundamental package for scientific computing in Python. It provides support for large multi-dimensional arrays and matrices, along with a collection of mathematical functions to operate on these arrays.

Let's say you want to calculate the mean and standard deviation of a dataset:

```python
import numpy as np

data = [10, 20, 30, 40, 50]
mean = np.mean(data)
std_dev = np.std(data)

print("Mean:", mean)
print("Standard Deviation:", std_dev)
```

NumPy makes it easy to perform complex numerical computations with just a few lines of code!

1.2 Pandas for Data Analysis

Now, imagine you're a data scientist exploring a large dataset containing information about customers. You need a tool to analyze and manipulate this data efficiently. Enter Pandas! Pandas is a powerful library for data manipulation and analysis in Python. It provides data structures like DataFrame and Series, along with functions to manipulate and analyze tabular data.

Let's say you have a CSV file containing customer data:

```python
import pandas as pd

# Load data from CSV file
df = pd.read_csv('customer_data.csv')

# Display the first few rows of the DataFrame
print(df.head())
```

Pandas allows you to read data from various sources, perform operations like filtering and aggregation, and visualize the results effortlessly!

1.3 Matplotlib for Data Visualization

Now, imagine you've performed some data analysis and want to visualize the results to gain insights and communicate your findings effectively. Matplotlib comes to the rescue! Matplotlib is a comprehensive library for creating static, animated, and interactive visualizations in Python. It provides a wide range of plotting functions to create various types of plots, including line plots, bar plots, scatter plots, histograms, and more.

Let's say you want to create a scatter plot to visualize the relationship between two variables:

```python
import matplotlib.pyplot as plt

# Sample data
x = [1, 2, 3, 4, 5]
y = [10, 15, 25, 30, 35]

# Create scatter plot
plt.scatter(x, y)
plt.xlabel('X-axis')
plt.ylabel('Y-axis')
plt.title('Scatter Plot')
plt.show()
```

Matplotlib enables you to create stunning visualizations with ease, making it an indispensable tool for data scientists and analysts!

Section 2: Introduction to Web Frameworks

2.1 Flask for Web Development

Now, let's switch gears and explore the world of web development using Flask! Flask is a lightweight and flexible micro-framework for building web applications in Python. It provides essential tools and libraries to create web applications quickly and efficiently. Whether you're building a simple REST API or a full-fledged web application, Flask has got you covered!

Let's create a simple "Hello, World!" web application using Flask:

```python
from flask import Flask

app = Flask(__name__)

@app.route('/')
def hello_world():
    return 'Hello, World!'

if __name__ == '__main__':
    app.run(debug=True)
```

With just a few lines of code, we've created a fully functional web application!

2.2 Django Basics

Next, let's explore Django, a high-level web framework for building web applications rapidly. Django follows the "batteries-included" philosophy, providing everything you need to build web applications out of the box. It includes features like an ORM (Object-Relational Mapping) for database interaction, a built-in admin interface, authentication, URL routing, and more.

Let's create a simple "Hello, World!" web application using Django:

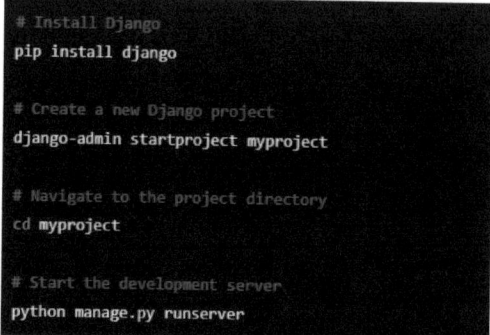

```
# Install Django
pip install django

# Create a new Django project
django-admin startproject myproject

# Navigate to the project directory
cd myproject

# Start the development server
python manage.py runserver
```

With Django, you can build robust and scalable web applications efficiently, making it a popular choice among developers worldwide!

Conclusion

Congratulations on completing Module 11 on Working with Libraries and Frameworks! You've learned how to leverage powerful tools like NumPy, Pandas, Matplotlib, Flask, and Django to enhance your Python programming skills. Whether you're performing numerical computations, analyzing data, visualizing results, or building web applications, these libraries and frameworks will be invaluable assets in your Python journey. Keep exploring and experimenting with these tools to unleash your full potential as a Python developer!

Module 12: Project-Based Learning

Welcome to Module 12! In this module, we'll explore the fascinating world of project-based learning (PBL). Project-based learning is an effective approach to education where students actively explore real-world problems and challenges through hands-on projects. By engaging in project-based learning, students not only gain valuable skills but also develop critical thinking, creativity, and collaboration abilities.

Section 1: Building a Simple Project

1.1 Understanding Project Planning and Design

Imagine you're tasked with building a simple inventory management system for a small bookstore. Before diving into coding, you need to plan and design your project. Let's break down the steps:

1. **Define Requirements:** Gather requirements from stakeholders (in this case, the bookstore owner) to understand what functionalities the system should have. For example, the system should track book titles, authors, quantities, and prices.
2. **Design Architecture:** Design the overall architecture of your system. Decide on the data structures and algorithms you'll use to implement the functionalities. For instance, you might use dictionaries or classes to represent books and their attributes.
3. **Create User Interface:** Design a user-friendly interface for interacting with the system. This could be a command-line interface (CLI) or a graphical user interface (GUI) depending on the bookstore owner's preferences.

1.2 Coding the Inventory Management System

Once you have a clear plan, it's time to start coding! Here's a simplified example of how you can implement the inventory management system in Python

```python
class Book:
    def __init__(self, title, author, quantity, price):
        self.title = title
        self.author = author
        self.quantity = quantity
        self.price = price

class Inventory:
    def __init__(self):
        self.books = {}

    def add_book(self, book):
        if book.title not in self.books:
            self.books[book.title] = book
        else:
            print("Book already exists in inventory.")

    def update_quantity(self, title, quantity):
        if title in self.books:
            self.books[title].quantity += quantity
        else:
            print("Book not found in inventory.")

    def display_inventory(self):
        print("Inventory:")
        for book in self.books.values():
            print(f"{book.title} by {book.author} - Quantity: {book.quantity}, Price: ${book.price}")

# Usage example
inventory = Inventory()
book1 = Book("Python Programming", "John Doe", 10, 29.99)
```

1.3 Testing and Debugging

Testing is a crucial step in the development process to ensure that our inventory management system functions correctly. We can write test cases to validate each functionality, such as adding a new book, updating quantities, and displaying the inventory. If any issues arise, we'll debug our code to identify and fix errors.

Section 2: Capstone Project

2.1 Choosing a Capstone Project

Now that you've mastered building simple projects, it's time to tackle a capstone project that integrates various concepts learned throughout this course. Let's brainstorm some exciting capstone project ideas:

1. **E-commerce Website:** Build a fully functional e-commerce website where users can browse products, add them to cart, and checkout securely.
2. **Health Tracker App:** Develop a mobile app that allows users to track their daily activities, such as exercise, nutrition, and sleep patterns.
3. **Smart Home Automation System:** Create a system that automates tasks in a smart home, such as controlling lights, temperature, and security cameras remotely.
4. **Financial Portfolio Manager:** Build a web application that helps users manage their investments, track portfolio performance, and analyze market trends.

2.2 Developing and Presenting Your Capstone Project

Once you've chosen your capstone project, it's time to roll up your sleeves and start developing! Throughout the development process, document your progress, challenges faced, and solutions implemented. Finally, prepare a comprehensive presentation to showcase your capstone project to your peers, instructors, and potential employers. Highlight the features, functionalities, technologies used, and lessons learned during the project development journey.

Conclusion

Congratulations on completing Module 12 on Project-Based Learning! By building simple projects and tackling a capstone project, you've gained valuable hands-on experience, honed your programming skills, and demonstrated your ability to solve real-world problems through code. Remember, project-based learning is not just about the end product—it's about the journey of exploration, experimentation, and growth as a developer. Keep coding, keep learning, and keep innovating!

Bonus Chapter 1:

Practice Exercises for Python Code Beginners

1. Write a Python program to print the sum of two numbers.
2. Write a Python program to find the factorial of a number.
3. Write a Python program to check if a number is prime.
4. Write a Python program to reverse a string.
5. Write a Python program to find the remainder when one number is divided by another.
6. Write a program that converts temperature from Celsius to Fahrenheit.

7. Write a Python script to concatenate two strings entered by the user.

8. Write a program to find the largest and smallest number in a list.

9. Write a Python program to generate random numbers between 1 and 100.
10. Write a Python program that handles division by zero and prints an appropriate message.

ANSWERS to Bonus Chapter 1

ANSWER 1

```python
num1 = 10
num2 = 20
sum = num1 + num2
print("The sum is:", sum)
```

ANSWER 2:

```python
def factorial(n):
    if n == 0:
        return 1
    else:
        return n * factorial(n-1)

num = 5
print("Factorial of", num, "is", factorial(num))
```

ANSWER 3:

```python
def is_prime(n):
    if n <= 1:
        return False
    elif n <= 3:
        return True
    elif n % 2 == 0 or n % 3 == 0:
        return False
    i = 5
    while i * i <= n:
        if n % i == 0 or n % (i + 2) == 0:
            return False
        i += 6
    return True

num = 17
if is_prime(num):
    print(num, "is a prime number")
else:
    print(num, "is not a prime number")
```

ANSWER 4:

```python
def reverse_string(s):
    return s[::-1]

string = "hello"
print("Reversed string:", reverse_string(string))
```

ANSWER 5:

```python
def find_remainder(a, b):
    if b == 0:
        return "Division by zero is not allowed"
    else:
        return a % b

# Example usage
num1 = int(input("Enter the dividend: "))
num2 = int(input("Enter the divisor: "))
print("The remainder is:", find_remainder(num1, num2))
```

ANSWER 6:

```python
def celsius_to_fahrenheit(celsius):
    return (celsius * 9/5) + 32

# Example usage
celsius = float(input("Enter temperature in Celsius: "))
fahrenheit = celsius_to_fahrenheit(celsius)
print(f"{celsius} Celsius is {fahrenheit} Fahrenheit")
```

ANSWER 7:

```python
def concatenate_strings(str1, str2):
    return str1 + str2

# Example usage
string1 = input("Enter the first string: ")
string2 = input("Enter the second string: ")
print("Concatenated string:", concatenate_strings(string1, string2))
```

ANSWER 8:

```python
def find_largest_smallest(numbers):
    largest = max(numbers)
    smallest = min(numbers)
    return largest, smallest

# Example usage
numbers = [int(x) for x in input("Enter numbers separated by space: ").split()]
largest, smallest = find_largest_smallest(numbers)
print("Largest number is:", largest)
print("Smallest number is:", smallest)
```

ANSWER 9:

```python
import random

def generate_random_numbers(n):
    return [random.randint(1, 100) for _ in range(n)]

# Example usage
count = int(input("How many random numbers do you want to generate? "))
random_numbers = generate_random_numbers(count)
print("Random numbers:", random_numbers)
```

ANSWER 10:

```python
def divide_numbers(a, b):
    try:
        result = a / b
    except ZeroDivisionError:
        return "Error: Division by zero is not allowed"
    else:
        return result

# Example usage
num1 = float(input("Enter the dividend: "))
num2 = float(input("Enter the divisor: "))
print("Result:", divide_numbers(num1, num2))
```

Bonus Chapter 2: Python Certification Prep Questions

Congratulations on your journey through this book! As a bonus, let's dive into some Python certification prep questions and practice exercises to solidify your understanding of Python programming concepts.

Python Certification Prep Questions

1. **What is the output of print(10 / 3) in Python?**

   A) 3.3333333333333335
   B) 3.33
   C) 3
   D) 3.0

   Answer: D) 3.0

2. **What is the result of the following expression: 7 ** 2?**

   A) 14
   B) 49
   C) 21
   D) 4

   Answer: B) 49

3. **What does the len() function do in Python?**

   A) Calculates the logarithm of a number
   B) Returns the length of a string or list
   C) Finds the largest element in a list
   D) Computes the square root of a number

   Answer: B) Returns the length of a string or list

4. **How do you access the third element in a list named my_list?**

   A) my_list[3]
   B) my_list(3)
   C) my_list[2]
   D) my_list(2)

   Answer: C) my_list[2]

5. **What is the output of print("Hello" + "World")?**

   A) HelloWorld
   B) Hello World
   C) HelloWorld
   D) Syntax Error

   Answer: A) HelloWorld

6. **How do you comment out a single line of code in Python?**

A) // This is a comment
B) # This is a comment
C) /* This is a comment */
D) <!-- This is a comment →

Answer: B) # This is a comment

7. **What does the input() function do in Python?**

A) Displays output on the screen
B) Reads a string from the user
C) Returns the current date and time
D) Converts a string to lowercase

Answer: B) Reads a string from the user

8. **Which of the following is a valid variable name in Python?**

A) my-variable
B) my variable
C) my_variable
D) my.variable

Answer: C) my_variable

9. **What is the correct way to declare a tuple in Python?**

A) my_tuple = (1, 2, 3)
B) my_tuple = [1, 2, 3]
C) my_tuple = {1, 2, 3}
D) my_tuple = 1, 2, 3

Answer: A) my_tuple = (1, 2, 3)

10. **What is the output of print("Python"[-1])?**

A) P
B) y
C) n
D) o

Answer: D) o

11. **What does the following code snippet do?**

```python
def greet(name):
    print("Hello, " + name + "!")

greet("Alice")
```

A) Prints "Hello, Alice!"
B) Prints "Hello, world!"
C) Raises a syntax error
D) None of the above

Answer: A) Prints "Hello, Alice!"

12. **How do you check if a key exists in a dictionary in Python?**

A) Using the contains() method
B) Using the exists() function
C) Using the in keyword
D) Using the has_key() method

Answer: C) Using the in keyword

13. **What will the output of the following code be?**

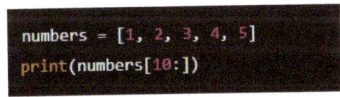

```python
numbers = [1, 2, 3, 4, 5]
print(numbers[10:])
```

A) [1, 2, 3, 4, 5]
B) []
C) [10]
D) Error: Index out of range

Answer: B) []

14. **Which of the following is not a valid method of the list class in Python?**

A) append()
B) remove()
C) pop()
D) sort()

Answer: B) remove()

15. **What is the output of bool("False") in Python?**

A) True
B) False
C) Error: invalid literal for int() with base 10
D) Error: bool object has no attribute 'False'

Answer: A) True

16. **What is the correct way to open a file named "data.txt" in Python for reading?**

A) file = open("data.txt", "r")
B) file = open("data.txt", "w")
C) file = open("data.txt", "a")
D) file = open("data.txt", "rb")

Answer: A) file = open("data.txt", "r")

17. **What is the output of 10 > 9 or 10 < 12?**

A) True
B) False
C) 10
D) 12

Answer: A) True

18. **How do you remove the last element from a list in Python?**

A) Using the remove() method
B) Using the pop() method with no index
C) Using the pop() method with an index of -1
D) Using the del keyword

Answer: B) Using the pop() method with no index

19. **What will the output of the following code be?**

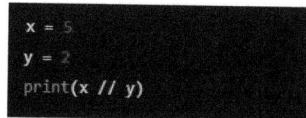

```python
x = 5
y = 2
print(x // y)
```

A) 2.5
B) 2
C) 2.0
D) 3

Answer: B) 2

20. **How do you convert a string to uppercase in Python?**

A) str.upper()
B) str.uppercase()
C) str.to_upper()
D) str.casefold()

Answer: A) str.upper()

Conclusion

Congratulations on completing this book! Throughout your journey, you've explored various concepts, developed new skills, and gained valuable knowledge. Let's review some key concepts and discuss the next steps in your learning journey.

1. Review of Key Concepts

1.1 Summarizing Key Points

- We've covered fundamental concepts such as programming languages, data structures, algorithms, and problem-solving techniques.
- You've learned how to apply these concepts to solve real-world problems through hands-on projects and exercises.
- We've emphasized the importance of clear communication, collaboration, and critical thinking in software development.

1.2 Reinforcing Understanding

- Take some time to review the key concepts presented in each module.
- Reflect on your learning journey and identify areas where you feel confident and areas where you may need further practice.
- Discuss concepts with peers or mentors to reinforce your understanding and gain new perspectives.

2. Next Steps

2.1 Further Learning Resources

- Consider exploring advanced topics and specializations based on your interests and career goals.
- Take advantage of online courses, tutorials, and workshops to deepen your knowledge in specific areas such as machine learning, web development, or cybersecurity.
- Stay updated with industry trends and best practices through blogs, podcasts, and conferences.

2.2 Introduction to Advanced Topics and Specializations

- Delve into advanced topics such as artificial intelligence, cloud computing, blockchain, and data science to expand your skill set and stay competitive in the ever-evolving tech industry.
- Explore specialized domains like game development, mobile app development, and embedded systems to pursue niche career paths.

Additional Resources

1. Reference Materials

1.1 Recommended Books

- "Clean Code" by Robert C. Martin
- "Cracking the Coding Interview" by Gayle Laakmann McDowell
- "Introduction to Algorithms" by Thomas H. Cormen
- "Design Patterns: Elements of Reusable Object-Oriented Software" by Erich Gamma

1.2 Online Resources and Communities

- Stack Overflow: stackoverflow.com
- GitHub: github.com
- Reddit: reddit.com/r/programming
- HackerRank: hackerrank.com

2. Practice Exercises

2.1 Coding Challenges

- LeetCode: leetcode.com
- CodeSignal: codesignal.com
- HackerRank: hackerrank.com/domains/tutorials/10-days-of-javascript

2.2 Real-World Scenarios

- Kaggle: kaggle.com
- Project Euler: projecteuler.net
- Exercism: exercism.io

www.ingramcontent.com/pod-product-compliance
Lightning Source LLC
Chambersburg PA
CBHW040759240526
45474CB00008B/120